GIANT VEHICLES
An Imagination Library Series

GIANT SCRAPERS

Jim Mezzanotte

GARETH**STEVENS**
GS
PUBLISHING
A Member of the WRC Media Family of Companies

Please visit our web site at: www.garethstevens.com
For a free color catalog describing Gareth Stevens Publishing's list of high-quality books and multimedia programs, call 1-800-542-2595 (USA) or 1-800-387-3178 (Canada). Gareth Stevens Publishing's fax: (414) 332-3567.

Library of Congress Cataloging-in-Publication Data

Mezzanotte, Jim.
    Giant scrapers / by Jim Mezzanotte.
       p. cm. — (Giant vehicles)
    Includes bibliographical references and index.
    ISBN 0-8368-4914-0 (lib. bdg.)
    ISBN 0-8368-4921-3 (softcover)
    1. Scrapers (Earthmoving machinery)–Juvenile literature. I. Title.
  TA725.M43   2005
  621.8'65–dc22   2005046910

First published in 2006 by
Gareth Stevens Publishing
A Member of the WRC Media Family of Companies
330 West Olive Street, Suite 100
Milwaukee, WI 53212 USA

Editorial direction: Mark J. Sachner
Editor: JoAnn Early Macken
Art direction: Tammy West
Cover design and page layout: Kami M. Koenig
Photo editor: Diane Laska-Swanke
Picture researcher: Martin Levick

Photo credits: Cover, pp. 5, 7, 9, 11, 13, 15, 19, 21 © Eric Orlemann; p. 17 © Urs Peyer

Printed in the United States of America

1 2 3 4 5 6 7 8 9 09 08 07 06 05

COVER: The Caterpillar company makes this giant scraper. It moves huge amounts of earth.

Table of Contents

Words that appear in the glossary are printed in
boldface type the first time they occur in the text.

Moving Earth

Giant scrapers dig and haul earth. They are big boxes on wheels. As a scraper moves, it scrapes the ground, scooping dirt. The dirt fills the box. When the box is full, the scraper leaves the dirt in another place.

Scrapers move a lot of earth. They usually move it a short distance. Scrapers help build roads, highways, and dams. They work at **mines**, too.

Giant scrapers are big and powerful. They have huge wheels for good **traction**. They have big engines. They are strong, too. They have to do tough jobs.

This giant scraper is hard at work. You can see its box filling with earth. When the box is full, the scraper moves to another place to unload.

Bigger and Better

The first scrapers were boxes made of wood. Horses pulled the boxes. Then **tractors** were built. The tractors pulled the boxes. They did a better job than horses.

In the 1930s, scrapers with engines were built. They did not have to be pulled. They could move on their own.

After World War II, people used scrapers a lot. In the United States, many highways were built. Scrapers helped build them. Scrapers got bigger. A big job needed a big scraper. The largest ones were built in the 1960s. Today, giant scrapers are still huge.

An early scraper is ready to unload. A tractor pulls this scraper. In later years, scrapers had their own engines. They became much bigger.

How Scrapers Work

The box that fills with dirt is called a bowl. The bowl has a gate at the bottom. The gate is called an apron. When the apron is open, dirt goes in. When the bowl is full, the apron is closed. The bowl is lifted so the scraper can travel. Then the apron opens. The load of dirt drops out.

How do you steer a scraper? It actually bends in the middle! The front and back are on a big hinge. When you steer, the whole front turns.

The back part holds the bowl. The front part holds the engine and cab. The front part pulls the back part.

The Terex company made this scraper. Earth goes into the bottom of the bowl. After the bowl is full, the apron will close. The whole front of the scraper turns.

Scraper Power

Scrapers have big **diesel** engines. The engines produce
a lot of **horsepower**. They use diesel **fuel**, not gasoline.
They have **turbochargers** for more power. For some jobs,
one engine is not enough. Some scrapers have two engines!
An extra engine in back turns the rear wheels.

A scraper has **hydraulic** cylinders. A cylinder is a big tube.
Inside, there is a smaller tube called a piston. Oil in
the cylinder pushes on the piston, and it slides out. These
cylinders raise and lower the bowl. They also open and
close the apron.

*This Caterpillar scraper has two engines! One engine turns
the big wheels in front. The other engine turns the big wheels
in back. These engines create a lot of power.*

How Big Is Big?

The LeTourneau company built the biggest loader of all time. It was called the LT-360. It was built in the 1960s. This loader had three bowls and eight engines! It was longer than a city block. It was so long, it looked like a train.

Today, giant scrapers are smaller. But they are still huge. Their big, fat tires are taller than most adults. They are four times as long as most cars. With a big load, they weigh more than eighty small cars. One load of dirt could fill many regular-size dump trucks.

This scraper is the LeTourneau LT-360. It was the biggest scraper ever built. Each engine produced more than 600 horsepower–and there were eight!

In the Cab

The cab is where you operate a scraper. It has big windows so you can see all around. It has a steering wheel, just like a car. It has pedals, too. There are **gauges** and lights. They let you know if anything is wrong. There are also many levers. They raise and lower the bowl. They open and close the apron.

In a scraper, you work long hours. You may work in bad weather. You have to stay comfortable. The cab keeps out noise and dust. It has heat and **air-conditioning**. The seat rides on a cushion of air. The cab may even have a stereo.

A scraper cab has a steering wheel and pedals. It also has many gauges, switches, and levers. The levers next to the seat control the bowl.

A Team Effort

Giant scrapers have good traction. But they can still get stuck. In some places, the ground is too hard to scrape. In other places, the ground is too muddy for the wheels. Steep hills can be a problem, too. The scraper gets help from other big machines.

A **bulldozer** often helps. It gets behind the scraper and pushes. Sometimes, two bulldozers line up in a row behind the scraper. Then they push at the same time. For other jobs, two scrapers work together. They link up like a train. Joined together, they have twice as much power.

Sometimes, scrapers need help. This scraper would get stuck if it worked alone. With the bulldozer pushing, it can get the job done!

Scraper Makers

The LeTourneau company made the first powered scrapers. Over the years, it made many scrapers, including the largest of all time. A lot of people used its scrapers. But it does not make scrapers anymore.

Today, Caterpillar makes giant scrapers. It makes other big machines for moving earth, too. The company has been around for many years. It is named after an early tractor that its **founder** made. People said the tractor looked like a caterpillar! The company makes giant bulldozers, **loaders**, and dump trucks. It makes different scrapers, from small to huge. The Terex company also makes big scrapers.

LeTourneau used to build some huge scrapers! This one has two big bowls. Today, the company does not make scrapers. But Caterpillar and Terex still do.

Scrapers at Work

Giant scrapers often help build roads. Roads have to be level. Scrapers take out all the bumps. Sometimes a road needs to go through a hill. Giant scrapers can get rid of the hill! They can even move the hill to another place.

Ready to work? First, you start the back engine. Then, you climb into the cab and start the front engine. A bulldozer gets behind you. You start moving. The engines roar. Dirt and rock fill the bowl. When the bowl is full, you close the apron. You raise the bowl. You speed away and dump the load. You are moving earth!

Operating a scraper is a hard job. You have to look ahead to watch where you are going. You also have to look behind to watch the bowl.

More to Read and View

Books

C Is for Construction: Big Trucks and Diggers from A to Z. Caterpillar (Chronicle Books)

Monster Road Builders. Angela Royston (Barron's)

Road Builders. Heavy Equipment (series). David and Patricia Armentrout (Rourke Publishing)

Road Builders. B. G. Hennessy (Viking)

Road Scrapers. Road Machines (series). Joanne Randolph (PowerKids Press)

DVDs and Videos

At Work With Heavy Equipment (Tony Nassour)

Big Toys (Library Video)

Heavy Equipment Operator: Cranes, Dump Trucks, Dirt Movers and More What Do You Want to Be When You Grow Up (series) (Tapeworm)

I Love Big Machines (Consumervision)

I Love Cat Machines (Caterpillar)

Web Sites

Web sites change frequently, but we believe the following web sites are going to last. You can also use good search engines, such as **Yahooligans!** (www.yahooligans.com) or **Google** (www.google.com) to find more information about giant vehicles. Some keywords that will help you are *Caterpillar scrapers, diesel engines, earthmovers, LeTourneau scrapers, powered scrapers, Terex scrapers,* and *Tournapull.*

auto.howstuffworks.com/diesel1.htm
This web site shows how a diesel engine works.

science.howstuffworks.com/hydraulic.
  htm
Visit this web site to learn more about how hydraulic machines work.

www.cat.com/cda/layout?m=37840
  &x=7&location=drop
At this web site, you can see many different Caterpillar machines, including giant scrapers. Choose "scrapers." Then choose a model by clicking on the model number. You can make the pictures larger. Click "Benefits & Features" to see more pictures.

www.tournanet.com/A%20pull.htm
Visit this web site to see a scale model of an early LeTourneau scraper.

Glossary

You can find these words on the pages listed. Reading a word in a sentence helps you to understand it even better.

air-conditioning (AIR-kun-dish-en-ing): a system that keeps a place cool when it is hot outside. 14

bulldozer (BUL-doze-ur): a vehicle with a big blade in front for pushing dirt, rock, and other things. 16, 18, 20

diesel (DEE-zull): the name for a kind of engine and the special fuel it uses. Most diesel engines are very reliable. They often use less fuel than gas engines. 10

founder (FOWN-dur): a person who started something, such as a company. 18

fuel (FYULE): something that burns to provide energy. 10

gauges (GAY-jez): devices that measure something, such as temperature. 14

horsepower (HORS-pow-ur): the amount of power an engine makes, based on how much work one horse can do. 10

hydraulic (hi-DRAW-lick): having to do with using water or another liquid to move something. 10

loaders (LODE-urz): vehicles that have big buckets in front for carrying loads. 18

mines (MINES): places where coal, gold, silver, and other things are taken out of the ground. Some mines are underground tunnels. Other mines are big holes, or pits. 4

traction (TRAK-shun): the grip that something has on a surface. To dig and carry heavy loads, a giant scraper needs a good grip on the ground. 4, 16

tractors (TRAK-turz): vehicles that pull things, such as a scraper bowl. 6, 18

turbochargers (TUR-boe-char-jurz): machines that force more air into an engine, giving it more power. 10

Index